# Pulled Pork in Paris

# Pulled Pork in Paris

Poems by

Athar C. Pavis

Cover design by Shay Culligan
Cover photo by Iena Shekhovtsova
Author photo by Robert Mitchell

ISBN: 978-1-63980-273-9

Kelsay Books
502 South 1040 East, A-119
American Fork, Utah 84003
Kelsaybooks.com

# Acknowledgments

*Able Muse:* "Ode to Silence"

*Alabama Literary Review:* "At the Market with Philip Roth," "Noces," "Dear Millennial"

*Avatar Review:* "French Windows," "Beggars of Montparnasse"

*Chariton Review:* "No Matter What They Meant"

*The Comstock Review:* "Mrs. Dalloway to D.P.," "Why the Camellia Won't Open," "He Asked"

*Explorations University of Alaska Press:* "Viagra Dreams"

*The High Window:* "Death of an Adjunct"

*The Lyric:* "Above the City," "Words"

*Measure:* "Below the Clouds"

*The Raintown Review:* "About the New Boss"

*The Road Not Taken:* "The Flirt"

*Slant:* "Rainbows of Sky," "The Mind at Last"

*Torrid Literature Journal:* "Lovers Who Might Have Been"

*Trinacria:* "What I Miss," "At the Chateau de la Chatonnière," "On Living in France," "There Is a Quiet Respite"

*Tule Review:* "In Defense of Dubai"

# Contents

# ANOTHER LIFE

# Second Summers

Their leaves have not turned yellow, and their limbs
still hold the fragrant smell of linden blossom—
reaching above the line of granite tombs,
they arch their trunks to sky, as if the autumn

could be outwitted. And the people too,
eager to find in their sidewalk cafés
a second summer, turn as the trees do,
imbibing sunshine. But these sunlit days

fade in and out above the cemetery.
Meanwhile along Montparnasse Boulevard
a man is roasting chestnuts, their sharp smell,
acrid and sad, their outer skins half-charred
remind of summer's passing—and how we
make second summers of impending fall.

# The Wardrobe Trunk

The wardrobe trunk my father bought
had seven tasseled drawers
and all the hanging space he thought
dresses would need. He was

partisan of the cocktail gown
cut low and long, the cloak
draping the shoulders, collared round
in iridescent mink.

He saw the trip I was to take
as one triumphant tour,
grand entrances, and Paris chic
in glamorous velours,

its bodice flounced in the soft pleat
of side swags at the waist—
not overdone, a sleek toilette
dominating the rest.

A little like Karenina,
he used to say, and smile—
complicitous and critical
of the beribboned frill.

And when the trunk was opened up
it stood at four feet tall,
a magic closet in a box
nobody knew was there,

its braided hangers made for silks,
plush drawers for lingerie,
the luxury a father thinks
I needed just to be.

And round the world it followed me,
Paris, Zurich, Rome,
but everywhere I went the trunk
came late, or didn't come.

Too late for countesses he knew
who took me to the Ritz,
operas they had tickets to—
or else the trunk would miss

whole cities I had traveled through
as each successive train
in a repeat scenario
brought every trunk but mine.

Perhaps because it was too big
to carry, and so full
no one could lift or even drag
the trunk alone, it would

arrive well after I had left,
instructed to proceed
to the next city, but the next,
already left behind.

I wandered cities on my own,
Naples, Syracuse,
the sky's immensity, Lausanne,
rose city, pink Toulouse,

without the trunk my father's care
had bought, filled to the brim
with all the best things to prepare
a life without him.

I sold the trunk when it reached Spain
in Barcelona Square,
and gave a smile to the three men
who'd dragged it there.

We celebrated with *tapas*
my freedom, so they thought,
but I still wonder what it was
my father bought

in buying that majestic trunk—
the dreams that were still his,
going to Saint Germain to meet
those countesses,

and what it was the trunk ensured
I would not risk or fail—
another life, as if he could
rewrite his own. But all

his plans fell by the wayside when
the trunk did not arrive—
I spent my days adrift with men
and I began to live

in many worlds, not just the one
of opera and ball,
Trastevere, the dregs of man,
and the worst men of all,

the pimps and parasites of girls
who prey on seeking hearts—
I learned to re-interpret words
where thinking starts,

and understood, despite my youth
those Trojan gifts
that lead the mind astray to doubt
evil exists.

And yet if I could be again
as I was once, I'd choose
blithe ignorance and that ball gown,
those ballerina shoes,

because the beauty of the world
is fleeting as the trunk,
before the mind can turn around,
too late to take.

Perhaps that's why he bought the trunk,
afraid I might miss out,
never to be that girl in me—
and he was right.

# Below the Clouds

I'll tell you what it's like: a Paris day,
grey on the blue-black roofs the fog has hid,
everywhere a mist of grey and more grey,
then suddenly a gold—the Invalide—

when I remember you. I see its dome
rising above the dimness of the hour,
gilding the sky and my abandoned home.
Beyond, the top of the Eiffel Tower

has broken off, but I am not undone.
The memory of you beneath the shrouds
of this dull day has brought a new surprise,
a light more splendid than the midday sun,
suffusing all: the soft light of your eyes—
because the sun has slipped below the clouds.

# Montparnasse Tower

Nobody likes the tower,
a Popsicle in the middle of Paris,
out of place, blocky, they say
even on its diagonal axis.

Something, though, happens at night
when strips of blank windows turn on,
like eyes opening to darkness
after grey days. Someone

is having fun notching its edges
in purple one night, then blue,
the tower, its masses made phantom
floats, as its blinkings undo

days of such solid beginnings,
certainties heavy as stone
in kaleidoscopes unexpected,
each night a different one.

Pulsating lights on its corners
erase all fifty-six floors,
blurred out, a building without them—
boxes the heart abhors—

so that for faces uplifted,
made phantom, the mass of it weighs
less than before, as new profiles
promise improbable days.

# The Problem With Me

*about the copropriété*

The problem with me is my French is too good,
I understand implicits, and my New York parts
seethe, as the make-believe of neighborliness
mouths a *bonjour*. The difference hurts.

The problem with me is I'll look for power
until I find it, as relentless as theirs,
a jackhammer to rip into the concrete
of these smug selves. Meanwhile careers

built on mere winning devour the mind,
law and jurisprudence, finance, I learn well
occupy the house where muses sang—
even to win can mean to fail.

So what's the choice? To stand up is still
an American value, to go out on a limb—
I know the law backwards, but what the soul says
goes silent. I have become them.

# On Living in France

Why, in a land where Liberty is touted,
Equality, Fraternity inscribed
on every public monument, men flout it—
and mavericks, who reach too high, proscribed?

Why fault the building super, who at six
puts out the garbage cans for half the square,
Stakhanovite, whose *self-made-man* heroics
bought him a future from his basement lair?

Why, when a man succeeds above his station,
there's no applause but quotes from La Fontaine,
this *know-your-place,* this scold whose French translation
means a mute class of less than equal men?

Why do they, hangdog, take it as their lot,
hauteur and put-downs by the hierarchy,
as if the age of reason, quite forgot,
yielded before this potent diarchy

of class and education *grande ecole,*
pearl necklaces, and clothes from *Franck et Fils*—
What is it in this way elites control
their underlings? As if a thought police

stomped out the smallest fire of ambition,
rewarding only absence of critique,
or those who speak, but not in contradiction
of any *supérieur hiéarchique?*

I've seen it in their faces as, obeisant,
they swallow hard at these indignities,
the way Madame Vaillant, bourgeois-complacent
reminds the building super that she sees

no reason why his bedroom is off limits
to the replacement person while he's gone,
his *loge,* his space, and everything that's in it,
obviously a *logement de fonction.*

I've seen it in the eyes a civil servant
lowers when asked for observations, yet
for anyone hierarchically observant
it's clear the invitation is a threat.

I never felt American till now,
as if I were a missionary here,
whose gospel is the dignity of how
these differences are not what they appear.

And being part outsider, and part in it,
a Martian to my hosts, uncategorized,
subversive, though I seem to some complicit,
I undermine hierarchical divide

if only for a moment, to suspend it,
to dream again, unbounded and, perchance,
awaken one who will go on to end it—
the future and the next best hope of France.

# Paris Nocturne

I walk the bridges of Paris at night
to remember who I am—
who knew a poet in another life
and all the sonnets of Petrarch.
You are the same.

The statues on the bridges stand alone
beckoning to the indifferent
and to us. We see their shadows better,
the dead, the dying, and our own,

what Henry the Fourth is smiling about
on his equestrian statue, turned green,
than our day selves. Five hundred years ago,
abjuring to become king,

did he renounce his faith and who he was
to live in the bold world of rank and power
but to remember, as the breath left him,
this evening hour?

# These Little Things

Sometimes to sit as the late hour sun
filters between the buildings, avenue Maine,
watching its rays slip past the Pullman Hotel,
gilding the room, as if in summer again—
can be enough. When they built that hotel,
a white colossus, its window-striped façade
obtusely rectilinear, they blocked out
three hours of winter light, but even so
an amber radiance infuses all, the dusk,
made briefer comes as luminous, to console—
these little things can sometimes be enough.

Meanwhile the hotel gutted from within,
breathing asbestos still, looms in the dark,
abandoned, a massive modern pyramid,
piled high beside it, the poison its walls hid—
and every hotel room its windows black.

# Beggars of Montparnasse

Maybe I should give to men
standing on street corners whose hair, unkempt,
brushes my face as I pass by—
I know how heavy it is on their shoulders.
*"Un petit sou, un petit sou,"* they say
softly. I keep walking with a hard face.
Maybe I should. They hold their cups out,
their eyes wavering, their mouths blurred,
their bodies bent. They hear it too—

something inaudible I've just heard
under the morning splendor of these skies—
and plumb like me unfillable space
within themselves. They know today
will be exactly the same as last night,
and every day the imprint of their pain
lies on them like blankets. But they smile,
whether or not I drop them a coin
because the money makes absolutely no difference.

# Sunset Surprise

*for A-S.*

To hope is a Parisian sky
lifting the gaze to see
horizons vaster than the eye
encompasses, to be

suffused in that pink stripe the sun
has painted on the clouds,
to celebrate, as if someone
had shaken off the shrouds

of this grey day and redefined
time lost as timelessness,
and happiness, a state of mind—
to hope is all of this.

Walk with me then, now unafraid
among these trees shorn bare,
boughs shivering on the Esplanade
as if in prayer.

And think of vistas still as bright
as these effulgent skies
as unexpected as the light
still in your eyes.

# Above the City

*at the Hôtel Raphaël*

On the roof of the Raphaël
one summer in September
I was the girl Chagall
painted to remember—

Mine was the mouth of rose
flying across the skies,
yours the blue suit that goes
above her as she flies.

High on the Eiffel Tower
arching beyond the Seine
something outside our power
lifted the clouds again

so that above Montmartre,
rose like a Shangri-la,
white Sacré Coeur made whiter,
horizons raised as high

as our sweet aspiration
in headlong flight—two hearts
a moment's hesitation
of colder logic parts.

Stay then with me forever,
image still incomplete,
absolute made lover—
eternity, concrete.

# The Man Whose Smile Embraced

*at the Copropriétaires meeting*

It's always the same: a pearl necklace,
a tailored suit, high heels—
look directly into the camera
of two hundred souls.

Especially if you disagree,
dress classic for the kill,
do not paint your fingernails,
sit perfectly still,

staring into the audience
as if each mouth you faced
were like the one in the seventh row,
the man whose smile embraced.

The man whose look and smile embraced,
who covers you with love—
someone like that in any row
is always good to have,

so that among two hundred there,
amid ill will and roar,
you and he, like accomplices,
have left to go somewhere,

a place where silence is a sound
and what his eyes said, word,
where nothing is as eloquent
as what no one has heard

but felt, as if a warming sun
a winter had replaced,
a sweetness rising in the room—
the man whose smile embraced.

# Dear Bruce

*Upstairs at Shakespeare & Company*


You can't have it both ways, you want the poem
to sound, but you're not interested in slam.
"It's gotta be poetic on the page"—
whatever that means, yet certain words are banned—
"disclose" and "comprehend," the Latinates.
"That's not how someone's gonna talk to me
on a bus," you said—and you were right.

But tell me how, if half the English tongue
is "rhetoric," vernacular can fill
these absences routinely unexpressed,
or bring a pause, as when above us still
hover the angels of our other selves
waiting to speak?  Don't get me wrong,

I use our conversations all the time
to mine in their demotic everyday
diamonds of self-deception, and I know
how the naming of parts, the humdrum noun
becomes something else. But when I see

dusk fall, rose-tinted over the blond stone
of Notre Dame, its beading all aglow,
as if each tower, suddenly bejeweled,
remembered color—when at dusk I hear
bells sounding deeply on the summer air,
time passing, softly, a piano played
in the next room, and all around me stand
books of dead authors high on these bookshelves
no one can reach—then, Bruce, I think of this,

what the conversational cannot express—
of Yeats' rose made sad, and metaphor,
of "silver-sandaled" stars you would reject,
of all those words, un-Twittered, un-Facebooked,
of souls who wait in vain to be unlocked.

# At the Chat Noir

*Spoken Word Night*


They'd chosen as the theme for *Spoken Word*
"First love, first time." Thinking of Turgenev,
and how to capture, in a stand-alone,
from a jerry-rigged stage, the basement crowd—
drinking their beers, but wanting a poem—
I remembered a tale I'd told myself,
summoning up the smell of frankfurters,
mustard and sauerkraut on Brooklyn streets,
pungent and sharp, and how that memory had
brought back to mind the Myrtle Avenue El,
the trash-strewn stoops, the men in undershirts,
the fenced-in courtyard Eastern District High
made "recreation period," and that day
I fell in love forever the first time.


A tale I'd told myself and memorized
to narrate on that night at the *Chat Noir*,
and it was sad, the way such stories are,
and I defiant, as if yesterday,
as if still smarting from the breach of it
I'd nevertheless decided to lay bare
the awful truth, difficult to accept
that first love is our last.
                          At the *Chat Noir,*
the beer was flowing freely, the MC
gesticulated grandly for applause
as readers came and went. And from the floor
a snickering rippled forth as the word "dick"
was mentioned, and the girl from Manchester
recounted in detail the slithering hands
doing vaginas hard in the back row.


33

The audience, transfixed, in loud guffaw
greeted each new audacity with "yeah,"
their eyes glazed over and their faces dull—
Beside me was a boy whose haunted air
reminded me that I was not alone.
How many others, having come to read
sat in stunned silence, as that basement room
titillated in a sordid bacchanal
of vicarious porn? Where are the words
we came here looking for, the kindred minds
who hear, beneath the surface, the unsaid,
altars defiled, the achingness that is
after the end? I turned to look around,
but nothing in the raunchy smile of some,
the gladsome gestures coming from the stage
comforted me. The boy by me had gone
and I, abandoned, blighted once again,
packed up my bags. I wasn't made for clubs.

And yet to tell even this beer-soaked crowd
the story of first love, may have found one,
a single listener listening to the poem,
and all the world redeemed because of him.

# I Can Live on Very Little

*for D.P.*

I can live on very little—
just a look, or the slow sweep
of the broom I hear soft-swishing
in a Paris half asleep,

A soft murmuring of morning,
each small miracle I see,
I can live on the high sparkle
of a moment, just for me,

as I cross the silent river
in the blackness of the night
and behold the Eiffel Tower
flash a thousand points of light.

I can live on just a glimmer
of the sun in the sunrise
not the kisses you would give her
but the kisses in your eyes,

not great vistas, but the angle
of the light upon your face,
I can live on the slight tremor
of your lips, and the embrace

never given, never taken,
but it's hard, as I have learned—
when the body is forsaken
how the soul itself seems spurned.

# Paris Tableau

*for Vincent*

I love the bells of Notre Dame
sounding the evening hour,
twilight rose-tinted on the stone,
ochre on alabaster,

horizons loosed from their grey lid,
the sun below the cloud,
and everywhere a sky that calls
the way my skies once did.

And this lost boy these Paris streets
have given a new voice,
who saunters forth a brave Rimbaud
I love, as in myself

I see, as if a second life
made possible in me,
the way this grey has changed to light,
changed utterly.

# CROSSROADS

# Why the Camellia Won't Open

Why the camellia won't open,
blossom bound in a tight ball,
lush leaves with nothing to show,
although the sap keeps rising—can be explained:
it sits in polished greenness on the sill
but for so many years it has not rained,
leaves shiny as if they were shellacked.
There is in the delicate embroidery
it does not have, a lack. Things we need,
absent too long, will atrophy
from underneath. The camellia won't bloom:
someone will have to come to save us both.

# The Crack

*after seeing Robert Redford's Lions for Lambs*

After the film they went about their business,
the old professor faded, and his words:
"Never again will you be the same person,
young, and a mind as open, but the choices
you make today will make you who you are."

And so the lesson both of them were hearing
was set aside, for they did not agree
on whether those two boys, by volunteering
became exemplars, their integrity
acting on their beliefs, and whether war,

even if wrongful, can lead men to greatness—
whether its killing fields can make men whole.
Instead he vented easy indignations—
a war, he said, that never should have happened—
while she cleared off the dishes and withdrew.

Because, I think, she'd heard the other message,
choices to make she could postpone no more,
how easily the present becomes future,
something ignoble she could not ignore,
and that the film was talking to her too.

# Viagra Dreams

Never marry a man without meeting
his father. Merchant, seer, or recluse,
he'll be the same as the prodigal son:
his face is his face. You think you know,

you live in a home with no doors—
how could you see? Only when you lie down
you hear it in your head, hear perfectly
something is breaking in the polished floors

like a varnish popped. And when you speak,
notice the eyes averted. Observe
he doesn't water the plants anymore.
What did you expect? What you deserve,

a hand lingering, a half-caress,
the way men look at women they undress
tenderly, and cover up to dream.
You cannot demand it. You must seem

satisfied. How did desire become
so many years ago, or by your fault
vulva of girls aglow, Viagra dreams,
flesh that meets pixel in a virtual heat?

You should have met his father. Men grow old
like the great pines to skyward, or bereft,
their branches orphaned, seek like some sad god
bodies to warm the bodies they have left.

# No Matter What They Meant

She put on her white dress half-sewn with pearls,
over-the-shoulder lace, a low-cut neck,
earrings of river pearl, and on her feet
sandals of silver straps embossed with jewels,
and wondered why only the others saw
her beauty, not the man she was living with.

Is it the kitchen detail dulls the eye,
the things to do, each unrequited care,
a broken vacuum cleaner, or the phones,
something to fix or something else to buy—
a man who doesn't see you anymore
become indifferent to the lives you wear?

Celebrate then, alone, each separate self,
mornings in the mist rising, hair unbound,
breathing the petaled phlox, a white nightgown
fluttering in the wind, and your arms bare,
the princess you become in those pink shoes,
the mermaid crowned with algae by the shore.

Better to live these variegated lives
than to rehearse a sullen discontent,
longings of inner selves, unrecognized
by the indifferent lovers we resent—
better to live each sobbing as our own
no matter what they meant.

# French Windows

It's early morning when she sees it best,
clearly outlined, three shadows on the wall,
windows that seemed like doors, now half-reduced,
high in their casements, the shadow of a cell

she'll have to leave. How did the sash become
a bar to hold her in, a beam, a weight,
and the French windows in her sunlit home
unopenable? Even if she gets out

mornings will always seem a shrunken space—
horizons vast as her Parisian sky
imprisoned here. In photo albums
she's put her house in order, expertly

slipping in their black pockets, one by one,
luminous days, for someone else to see.

# This Is as Good as It Gets

Whoever you are who pass me in the street,
whose smile is like a warm sun on my shoulders,
sweet, like the smell of orchids in the rain—
what does it matter whether or not we meet

again? As if a life lived out,
mornings of packaged cereals, days on end
of details, could attract more than this flame,
instant of recognition still the same

forever? This is as good as it gets.
and so I live where some can only dream
evenings of inevitable pork chops.

# The Flirt

*Francis Huster et al.*

"Beautiful eyes," he said, the usual,
a man sure of himself, the way men are,
lifting his handsome face to gauge effect,
declaiming how the seats in the fourth row
gave the best view and wouldn't hurt the neck.

He wore an Ascot just the way she liked,
its flouncing blue, a shirt of cotton sheer,
his cheeks were taut, and his regard intense,
rueful a bit, his mouth, as if he knew
seduction was just another role of his.

And yet he was observant, paid his due
to beauty as he saw it, dreaming still
another life, made possible in her,
albeit for a moment—something new,
before she turned away and left him flat.

But left him flat for what? A man who gives
a measuring cup for Christmas, practical,
a partner who remembers the gas bill,
never to gaze at her the way he did.
So, in her secret chambers, she relives

that moment in *Blood Diamond* the doomed man
looks at the only woman he has loved,
or Lensky singing *ya lyublyu vas,*
and thinks next time one word might be enough
even if it's just a flirt, to save her life.

# Not for Him, the Ribbon in My Hair

*Dialogue at the Quai d'Orsay*


Not for him, the ribbon in my hair—
What made him think it was?
"The hierarchy, no doubt. Beware,
he is the *universe,* because

he graduated from somewhere,
a habit of the mind, I think.
Haven't you noticed how we hear
him holding forth, but just to speak

of him, himself, and never how
you came to be?"—It's true, but he
has a fine mind, surely must know
people are more than he can see.

"Ah, my poor friend, such naïveté
will cost you dear. In him there pants
an opportunist in his day
who spends his time with sycophants,

a man accustomed to cliché,
an Epicure above reproach
who sips Chassagne Montrachet
and does not see or think too much

of others who, misunderstood,
like obstacles he will pass by,
or pause, the way a driver would—
something, perhaps, has caught his eye

to pick, and smell, and throw away
and never hear the sob beneath.
You're but the perfume of a day
plucked from a wind-blown heath

whose sweep and fall he cannot hear—
What did you think? The Little Prince?
Beware his cufflinks and beware
silk ties that bind. Not ever since

childhood has he re-met the rose
or bent to hear the river speak.
He has his coffee, and he goes
about his business. You mistake

good taste for passion. So your hair
beribboned was *for him,* as were
the whispers rising in the air
he passes through: 'Bonjour, Monsieur

l'Ambassadeur,' and, like them, you
are pleasing, and one reverence more
in the wide world that is his due.
I think you should desist before

you are seduced, as you will be."
Not him, nor any man can slake
desire an absence burns in me,
and if it is a risk I take

I'll wear my ribbons anyway,
to celebrate myself alone
so men remember what I say
before my mouth has turned to stone

and my green eyes are gone, or dulled
the light illumining my face—
a courtesan no man has loved
whose dreams no lover can debase.

# Letter to Onegin

*for D.P.*

Why should I love you, if to hear you say
matter of fact, as you referred to her:
"I'm ending the relationship"—to be
plucked for display, disposed of like a weed.
To see tomorrow clearly is to see
these pauses in your life as may occur
between assignments of more pressing need.

So wandering, inconstant, and away,
a new Onegin come upon my heart,
do not expect indulgence: I do not
believe you for a moment, but can read
upon your lips the lips your own have sought,
the absences your presences impart,
the little pile of secrets you still hide.

It's hard to draw conclusions either way—
maybe a broken heart is better off
than certainty of pain before the fact.
Why should I love you as so many have
except to find, still trusting and intact—
as if the aspiration were enough—
myself again in everything I gave.

# I Don't Want to Be Told Good-bye

I don't want to be told good-bye
the way they do in France
sometimes for the sake of pure form,
or when they're in a hurry.
Don't put out one cheek, and then the other,
give me at least a lingering kiss—
or don't bother!

# Words

Better say nothing than to say
*Je vous trouve très sympathique,*
packaged phrases Frenchmen say
so not to speak . . .

Who could have said the world is hard,
grey the sky, and cold the earth,
but in the warmth of your regard
a sweet rebirth . . .

And if so daring you had been
my own redemption might have won
from silence, and my mind again
and heart been one.

And held you to me like a kiss,
and covered you with wings
as tender as the tenderness
of unsaid things.

until the words you would have found
like blossoms, fell in ways
more beautiful than flowers bound
in rich bouquets.

# There Is a Quiet Respite

*for D.P. l'ardent sanglot at the Hôtel Raphaël*

There is a quiet respite in the hour,
a solace, a repose, when I see you
as if, unknown to us, another power
had drawn a velvet curtain, and it drew

around us like a blanket. From afar
we hear a muffled echo of the world,
and in the sweet oasis of the hour
we hear a murmur we have never heard.

A sound of the soul's sobbing, like a wind
rustling still within us like a prayer,
rising in ardent sadness to a hymn,
desperate, and yet indifferent to despair.

It is as if, companions in a sorrow,
a weight is lifted from us, and the cry
—Console me, I am inconsolable—
made bearable, dissolves into a sigh.

As if, in the implacable decree
of busy days, and futile enterprise
we hear the rush of music in the sea
lifting its wave to sunward as it dies.

And you and I, each stranded on a beach,
asunder and together, feel the heave
of tides to islands we can never reach,
of lives to earthward we can never leave.

# Lovers Who Might Have Been

He must have seen, even against the light
the trace of crow's feet, a droop in the mouth,
a flaccid look about the neck, and jowls
waiting to appear. Her cheeks had fallen

but still in homage to her youth she wore
heeled boots laced high in the new retro style,
a dress of jersey knit molding her form,
a low neckline. I think he saw her

for the first time, the way a woman sees
she has grown old, out of the blue, betrayed
by what the mirror says, and his youth too,
twice lost because of what he thought he'd had—

a lithesome girl. And so he let her go
with no good-bye and no regret. He would,
he thought, forget, and so he did. But when
night comes, he sometimes wonders how her braid

would look undone, and whether other men
are with her now, while she does what she can.
And so they wait, lovers who might have been,
he for perfection, she for another man.

# Mrs. Dalloway to D.P.

Even if in the end nothing new can be invented
and touch implodes, to leave a sunless planet,
surfeited men, blankets of airless air—
this incandescence is its own reward.

I take it back, therefore, what I told you then,
having lived too long with sheets stretched tight
on narrow beds. I take it back. And I will say—
the very next time, if ever again

I feel your eyes upon my face,
your warmth made radiance in me—
I didn't understand these sunlit days
are all we have. Light-years from now,

after the glow has left them, we will gaze
and see them still, the way astronomers,
luminous, in some far-off galaxy,
observe a virtual light that is no more.

If then, our cosmic paths should cross again,
love me, that we remember who we were
eons from now, like supernova stars
long dead, still burning bright on blackening skies.

# The People I Love

The people I love are like the trees
on Alésia, their limbs chopped off,
looking as if no sap moves them
toward Spring. But underneath
vague aspirations coursing in their blood
conjure a wilder heath.

The people I love are like Satie,
smooth, but a sob still caught beneath
a pool of music crystalline and clear—
who would have thought someone was there?

And you who have revealed today
another self, out of control
over a bottle of Beaujolais,
I love like theirs your wayward soul.
Moody you are like this March day—
and beautiful.

# After the Garden Party

The last time I saw you
in cufflinks and tie
I could have invented
something to say—

the factoids we garner,
the memes we dispense,
anything, really
the mind invents.

Instead I kept distance
and my yellow dress
walked in the garden
with someone else.

Unwilling to network
glib with champagne,
I guard remembrance
to live again—

the summer I met you,
the light in your eyes,
the soul's recognition
in mute surprise,

tender, uncertain
like the softest breeze,
carrying the fragrance
of unnamed trees,

tentative as music
played faintly somewhere
wavering, recurrent,
a wistful air

somehow familiar
but not heard before,
a piano playing
behind a wall,

How in these moments
if you'd been as brave
life re-imagined
was ours to have.

If now you send me—
since nothing occurred—
professional mailings
I haven't read

don't ask me to "follow,"
invite me to join,
"Friend" you tomorrow
where you have gone.

I live in a castle
unopened for years
whose drawbridge is broken,
moated with tears.

High on the towers
crenellated stone
I meet on the ramparts
myself alone,

and from this bastion
observe on the plain
Lilliputians passing
who call my name.

# Pulled Pork

The man holding the flowers who offered me his seat,
his hat askew, something like an artist,
his features gaunt, just the way I like them,
insisted, when I turned away, embarrassed . . .

It could have been he saw my cheeks had fallen
under hyaluronic acid, or the brow,
furrowed beyond repair Botox injection
promises us, the bald hairline, or how

the catastrophic failure to express love
changes a face like something life has used,
cooked long and slow like pulled pork on a stove
until connective tissue is destroyed—

It could have been, or maybe even now
he sees in my green eyes a new believing,
my Botticelli pose, a poem—I doubt it, though,
the neck as it grows old is unforgiving.

You splash a greying hair with *Lady Grecian,*
you cream away the crow's feet by your eyes,
but even if you fool the people looking
something in you, like pulled pork, never lies.

The winsome future your face offers up,
another life made possible, will dim,
blank out, and like a curtain lifted, drop—
your only future waits for you within.

Put on your pretty faces, your mascara,
accentuate your eyes, so none detect
how the lip turns in corner lines still lower,
a mouth that warps to hold the heart in check.

No matter how, to exorcise the evil—
in age-defying uplifts, or massage—
of beauty robbed, we improvise or fail to,
materially we know it's a mirage . . .

And yet I like to think it was this face,
something still in my eyes and in my look,
that made him turn to offer me his place,
and made him give the flower that I took.

# SALARYMAN

# About the New Boss

*reply a colleague at the Quai d'Orsay*

It's not so easy to write someone off—
There's more to him than default mode, though less,
perhaps, than I imagine. The right stuff,
sycophant or director, you insist,

rarely survives. Still, he's not what he seems—
anyone who writes poems on weekends can't
live just his public face —the poem reclaims
a part of him his day job shutters out.

Dictator in the office, he can hear
rain on the windowsill, and in the trees,
how the wind buckles, bends their branches low
until they snap. He knows what grief is,

walks in the cemetery of Montparnasse,
remembers poems, and where the poets are
who move him still. You think because he has
no obvious pain to show, you can be sure

he's nothing but indifference, and that we,
sensitive souls, seem nothing to his rank—
Caligula, you say, wrote poetry,
and Nero too, and yet I cannot think

of any man the way you do, defined
by what is outer and observable—
I'd rather be mistaken and maligned
for naïveté, the way discoverers were

before they found—in drawings on a wall—
proof of an inner life, in rapt surprise
and recognition in Neanderthal
a part of themselves. Something human dies

if I cannot believe, beneath the mail,
there lives and breathes another heart like mine,
as if it were not he, but I who fail
to summon forth a life that might have been.

# On Being Offered Pay for Lessons Not Given

The French social conscience is offensive—
You tell me, "But I will sign . . ."
and I, who in these conversations
saw myself Socrates, am to be paid
even if the conversation does not take place.

French social conscience reduces the exchange
as if the question of the questioner—
a sudden stop, a stillness in the room,
our certainties cascading like a house of cards—
were one half hour to be remunerated . . .

Humbling it is, your carefully kind offer
reminding us how little we mean
despite this incandescence, to each other—
occasional grace reduced to the paid hour.
How hard I think it must be to remain
prisoners of the jobs you think we are—

So don't expect the intellect to soar,
unfettered and irreverent, the same wit
if it's for money that I'm doing it—

the French social conscience is a bore!

# At the Quai d'Orsay

It doesn't matter who you are,
the extra mile, the things you've done,
how many times your presence there
opened itself to everyone.

In this environment you've been
a *"formateur"* and nothing more—
they pay the hours you put in
and think that's what you're working for.

Superimposed upon it all,
the hierarchy is in command
that you, like some strange animal
do not appear to understand.

They say the word caressingly,
*"hiérarchie,"* and in the sound
you hear their reverence and see
their bodies set to sweep the ground

to bend and bow, obsequious,
servile, and you still mystified
why they consider serious
some hierarchical divide.

You see debate as mutual,
but for them you're an employee,
talented but dispensable—
to discuss is to disagree.

Whatever, or how you say it,
if not what the kinglets expect
seems outright insubordinate—
a proof of your disrespect.

So call up that line from Chaucer,
to "gladly teche"—what you've sown,
after is all that will matter,
your life for itself alone.

How it stood fast in contention,
irrespective of rank or blame,
how this is its own redemption—
the woman that you became.

# On Mandating One Minute of Silence

*the Minister orders one minute of silence*
*after the murder of Samuel Paty*

"OK, so you want to ram it down our throats—
But is it really about the Prophet?
Freedom of speech and the Republic—
this caricature you keep insisting on?
As if the Muslim piety it flouts
were nothing else? My brother mows their lawns,
my mother cleans their toilets, scrubs their floors,
and you imagine 'secularists' repeating
the mantra of the State? There's something more
lurking beneath these cartoons of 'free speech'—
       the hate they teach."

"But that's absurd. It's just the right to say
whatever we think, there's nothing off limits,
least of all religion in the land of Voltaire—
we're secular—and we fought hard for it,
decades, in fact, before the Church lost sway.
But you, because you're 'politically correct,'
would muzzle freedom with a false respect—
freedom is what the Republic is about,
no matter what. And Muslims must expect
rights, and the duties too, we will enforce,
       on all, of course."

"Rights, and the duties too, you will enforce,
as if there were no room for differences—
that rapper you found unacceptable,
what happened to his sacrosanct 'free speech'?
Tell me if I break silence with my voice
next Monday, will you practice what you preach—
allow my 'minute of silence' as my own
or force a public grief put on display
to prove me French? I am a citizen,

66

you say, where no 'communities' exist—
        except the State.

"And this is why burkinis aren't allowed
in swimming pools, or halal food, for lunch,
even in cafeterias at ZEP schools,
why headscarves must be jettisoned at the door—
You call this secularism? Or is your crowd
just pigeonholing, as we've seen before,
when women were denounced as terrorists
for how they dressed? I'll tell you what you are:
bigots, secular fundamentalists,
fierce as Inquisitors of a new religion—
        who can't imagine

how anyone might need identity."
"Identity is whole, not hyphenated
you're French or not, there's nothing in between—
and when you are, our values are your own."
"What does this mean, that I cannot be me,
that being French I must perforce disown
hijab, abaya or my father's land?
And in exchange for what? Frisked every day,
half-citizen, half suspect, faith maligned,
forced to pay homage to a caricature
        of who I am?"

They quarreled again, each could not see the other.
The State in France has something of Robespierre,
Enlightenment that rubs their noses in it—
meanwhile a future Allahu akbar
is growing up to vindicate his brother.
Somewhere on the horizon there's a war
we can't see yet, while idly from his cave,

heaving his hungry maw a monster stirs
cauldrons of body parts, and pundits rave—
refusing all refusals or to stomach
    this threat to the Republic.

# The Day I Asked Them Who They Were

Usually I don't ask, I go forward,
there are so many needs, things to get done,
basic infrastructure, irregular verbs—
they've never heard of GAAP, the SEC—
and we're studying fraud, Enron, WorldCom,
how once you start down that slippery slope,
creative accounting, cooking the books,
it's hard to come back. They listen to me,

suddenly attentive, as if someone
already remembered, already saw
into the future, a weakness, and how
they too might fail. Generally I ask
questions, but only about the case—
a tremor in the lips, a front-row face
brought me up short. I invited them all
to a rooftop lunch on top of the town,

a rooftop, the school's, where they'd never gone—
above the clipped park where horizons unfurl
a panorama of the possible
become theirs too. "So where are you from?"
I asked as they selfied the Eiffel Tower:
"Senegal, Cameroun, Burkina Faso,"
they laughed as they added Clichy-sous-Bois,
the projects of Creil, Saint-Denis, Pierrefitte,

the hours it takes for their commute.
Yesterday, walking by a vacant lot
I thought of them all, how the tangled weed
smothering the ground, the bushes, the trash,
barriers graffitied, still couldn't stop
four poppies growing across the fence
and—in the middle of that choked terrain—
red clover rising to bloom again.

# On Persuading André to Run for President

In attitude we don't agree,
you take the hierarchy to heart—
we both know what the world should be
but you are French, and I am not.

Tell me how we can move the earth,
how we can bring the sun to bear
on countless minds, and in one breath
kindle a fire that was not there

if you, before the spark is lit,
believe yourself the lesser
because, though he's a hypocrite,
he's still a full professor!

And how can you, who know the world,
imagine, once in power,
he could be deputy-controlled
by you—he will devour

your soul, horizons still in you,
rainbows you cannot yet express,
and nothing in you will ring true
but what seemed more . . . will become less.

# Conversations with Gérard Lapierre (1)

*Paris after Madrid*


You would have laughed to hear them say
the bombs exploding in Madrid,
the bodies ripped apart, the grey
ashes of limbs, the slick of blood

on burning streets, was Judgment Day.
"Judgment of what?" I hear you scoff,
as if a fire goes away
when people simply cry: enough!

"And do you think," you would pursue,
"Paris aloof, behind its gates,
politically correct, like you,
whose Minister commemorates

the dead and dying, still well-coiffed,
can keep the country safe for us?"
"France will be French," they would retort:
"No hyper power calls the shots."

Oh, palaces intact and proud
behind escutcheons still agleam,
grilles where a thousand men stand guard,
this calm is not what it may seem . . .

You would have said, if you were here.
Nothing can ever be undone—
and worlds exploding everywhere
die like your world, in everyone.

# Conversations With Gérard Lapierre (2)

"Let me explain," you liked to say
the day the Eiffel Tower turned red
or Christmas trees in body bags
littered the streets. You had

an explanation for everything
the war, or why the interest rate
was kept sky-high at the ECB,
the price of oil, or what

Trichet did when he cooked the books
in the name of France. You told me
"I would have done it myself."
Crises you could foresee

came and went at the Bank of France.
Behind that double padded door
you were never surprised. You knew
everything but never saw

in the dark hallways of the Bank
where Mercury is caught in stone
a labyrinthian corridor
beckoning where you have gone.

"Let me explain," I want to hear,
why you who knew the way by heart,
who slew the dragons lurking there
could not get out . . .

# Tell Me Another Story

*la monarchie republicaine*


They talk a good game, hell-bent
on poking fun at power,
Pope or Prophet, President
lampooned—the Gallic ire

bucking all authority,
spoofing their pomp to jeer
fervor—or hypocrisy—
thumbing their nose at fear.

But, have you ever seen them,
adepts of *Charlie Hebdo,*
holding their tongues at meetings
even though most of them know

bosses can be mistaken,
misguided or misinformed—
doubts, though, remain unspoken,
an intricate rite performed,

whereby hierarchical presence
mysteriously subdues
rebels to strange obeisance,
refuseniks, who won't refuse,

the mind become a servant,
obsequiously alert,
hovering, but abeyant
beneath a bow-tied shirt,

nodding assent, arm-napkined,
deferent in its reserve,
awaiting to be given
signals for what to serve.

Pity the heart half-muffled
whose every breath is bound,
indignities soul-suffered,
whose being has not found

a path to that high kingdom
of wholeness in all things,
whose mind is held in ransom
to passing office kings.

Honor, in random access,
still blinking on and off,
whose motherboard is broken
reminds him of himself.

Harder than mocking pundit,
marching for freedom of speech,
the daily living of it
makes heroes of us each.

Praise then unfailing candor,
oblivious of rank,
philosophers forever
allergic to group-think

so that, for the faint-hearted,
hierarchical divide
in hearts subordinated
a fire has not died.

Tell me another story
of courage every day,
the soul that dares endure it,
the mind that dares to say.

# The Pedagogical Advisor, Quai d'Orsay

She had a fresh air to her; her long hair—
a jacket, yes—but, still, the jeans she wore,
her leather boots, a slinky blouse cut low,
made her "informal" to the group. She knew
how to talk shop with teachers, how to speak,
opening doors—it seemed—to their ideas,
insisting, as a *conseiller pédagogique*
she wasn't administration—she was free,
advising them at meetings quite apart,
brainstorming them together as a team,
appointed, yes, by hierarchy, but at heart
she'd been a teacher once, they were "the same."

She wore no make-up and her earnest look,
clearly unstudied, gave them hope she would
tame the bureaucracy she undertook
to interface on their behalf. She gave
cluckings of acquiescence, their complaints
acknowledged, a commiserating smile
stamped on her lips, upon her limpid brow
an innocence, as if she shared their will
to gladly teach. And so they told her how
under the yoke of modules by machine,
robotized tests, students pigeonholed,
no sudden talent, hidden, unforeseen

could burst upon them: students might have been
better than what they scored computer-tested,
freed from their fear, but clearly this might seem
subversive to a system so invested
in measuring not potential but a floor—
the lowest common denominator
of competence. So what were teachers for,

unless by strict parameters defined
to lower all horizons—and their own?
She listened as they told her how this meant
the end of pedagogical surprise,
tethered to a digital straitjacket

teachers might toe the line of compromise,
ranking the students so their orals fit
computer scores. If she could intervene
they wouldn't have to fight this fight alone,
for even she could see how the machine,
inaccurate, diminished everyone
to what was only measurable amount.
She listened, nodding, seeming to consent
the point, and yet six months passed by the same,
somehow the oral scores the teachers sent
began to mirror the computer grade
as their advisor, too, no longer came

alone to meetings, but with boss in tow.
And so it is that imperceptibly
the self that is the self we think we know
bends to the wind prevailing, like the reed.
She never saw how slowly she became
servile and hard, in spite of her blue jeans,
the mouthpiece of administrative rule,
her essence lost, her candor undermined.
I've heard if we can call things by their name
we break the spell some people use to fool
themselves into acceptance, but who dared?
Cowards, they let her sink, and no one cared.

And so it can be argued they deserved
their own abasement which soon followed hers.
Teachers had tasks, timetables to respect,
no time for pedagogical debate—
just get the tests online, she once observed
and shut your traps. In truth, in her defense
she had a calendar to think about,
a road map, efficiency measurement,
process she couldn't change, and a format
imposed by high hierarchical decree—

And so it is how the once passionate
become, like her, no more than employee.

# Who You Are

*for Remi at the Quai d'Orsay*

Pity the man who sees as his career
subservience to a political master,
how much he will anaesthetize to bear
his own aliveness, as if it didn't matter.

So young, a mind awake, a soul still brimming,
may you dream still, not kowtow to another,
so that your face at thirty-five, believing,
will still be yours, observing from the mirror.

Who was it said we are responsible
after that age for who we have become—
pity subaltern hearts no hope will kindle,
yes-men whose worldly wisdom has undone.

You think at work you'll have to be pragmatic,
to pander to ideas you don't believe,
performing more than living, diplomatic,
as if at five o'clock you will retrieve

yourself, intact and pure. But something happens.
Listen to me, I know, for I have seen
aspiring hearts reduced to face-time flunkies,
a man who put a bullet through his brain.

Observe the unctuous courtier, but remember
*You are the one you have been waiting for,*
the light bright in your eyes your only measure
because how you spend your days is who you are.

# Requiem

*at the Quai d'Orsay, Paris*

They started young; a Foreign Minister
demanded action, so their mission grew,
languages now topping the agenda—
no one had learned them properly at school.

They started young, Aglaia and Gonzalez
who brought Oswaldo in. The Ministry,
eager to bolster its linguistic levels,
turned a blind eye to who brought who, and why.

A matter of the highest state importance,
teachers were given freedom, and the care
of course design, materials, distribution,
of who did what, and how the *fonctionnaire*

became, from false beginner, diplomat.
It was a heady time, though teachers were
adjuncts, and in that state, a world apart
from civil servants whose pay, regular,

remunerated whether they worked or not.
Aglaia and the others made decisions
all on their own, they were not paid if sick,
but set, without the usual supervisions,

the dates of their vacations. They were free.
Free also from hierarchical divide,
of *concours*-driven Category B,
and from the social prejudices that hide

beneath the smile a Category C
gets from a B before her words betray
she's a Cat C, just cleverly disguised—
pearl necklace, suit, seemingly Quai d'Orsay—

a pretty fraud, in fact. Aglaia'd heard
tale upon tale of hierarchy and how
someone she'd taught, that very day, who feared
he'd fail a second time the *concours A*

put a bullet through his brain. Teachers stood
outside this system steeped in protocol,
and even if they knew the deference due
superiors, pretended not to know.

However bureaucratic or coercive,
they knew their bosses, in three years, would leave,
and "ignorant," they could remain subversive,
biding their time, awaiting their reprieve.

And so it was that they were seen as Martian,
as *gauche,* or uninformed, for any breach,
American, Irish, even German,
beyond the fear of bureaucratic reach.

They made the rules for peer-to-peer recruitment,
on how to test each language, for they knew
Italian was too easy, comprehension
couldn't be weighted the same way they do

in languages like English. But one time,
a boss, nicknamed Napoleon, did require,
for two long years, till they got rid of him
(his new assignment to Bulgaria),

uniform weighting and an online test.
And once he called her in, a teacher said,
*"convoquée,"* and bidden to change a course,
to give it to a friend of his instead.

80

Claiming she had no power, she told him
caressingly, "Of course you are the boss—
you can change this, but then the teaching team
might not understand." She saw him pause,

and all his paintings of Napoleon
purse their lips. Someone had taught her well—
seemingly docile, saying he's the one
to make decisions, she could play the fool,

as if she didn't know his secret shame—
that he'd back down, as bosses always would
without subordinates to take the blame.
And that is how it ended, what he did.

In the Ministerial scheme of things
Aglaia and the others were bright spheres,
planets as unpredictable as those
outside the ordered universe, and theirs

a world outside a world of low intrigue,
where in their classes students could retrieve,
freed from the prison of their native tongue,
a self unfettered and a soul alive—

a self apart from rankings that defined
identities, the Ministry's *Who's Who,*
by which they were each sorted and assigned
to their respective stations, and to show

proper respect above, if none below.
Here, in another language, they were free,
ambassadors could sing, prefects recite
*"It fell so low in my regard,"* and be

wide-eyed and young again, rebellious, true.
More than just language-learning, it was air
whispering low, a rustling of leaves
reminding them of sky, a sudden stir,

a wayward wind uplifting a dropped sail,
a call to open vistas and wide seas,
another life new syntaxes reveal
as possible—no overlings to please,

only the secret orders of the heart,
the aspirations of another time,
old curiosities they had forgot,
the dignity of being what they seem.

As if, above the dull grey blanketing
autumnal dome of heavy mist and cloud,
they saw again through a brief opening
halo of bright horizons they once had,

radiant as unexpected light
seen through the funnel of their narrow days,
luminous, as when clouds separate
gilding all Paris in a golden glaze.

Aglaia and the others opened rooms
long closeted, their couches draped in cloth,
windows that wouldn't open to the wind—
where language still unpolished spoke the truth.

And all went well, since what the teachers gave
no one could put a finger on, yet seemed
the oxygen that freer spirits have,
another life, unlived but not undreamed.

Until Aglaia suddenly fell ill,
brutally ill, a tumor like a plant
growing in her, something unnamable,
cancer of the vagina—and she quit.

The chemo made her bald, she couldn't teach,
too weak to work, she was left penniless,
adjuncts just being paid for hours clocked,
she lived on friends' donations. It was this

that brought to mind the project she took on.
She would reform a system that relied
on adjuncts, to make salaried everyone—
security that civil servants had

would be the teachers' too. A militant,
she knew just how to organize and lead—
this was the legacy if nothing else
she'd leave her colleagues even if she died—

her life would have a meaning, an effect.
They rallied to her as her body failed,
their promises more sacred with her death—
they fought the Ministry, and they prevailed,

each of them got a contract, they were safe.
And yet a new anxiety took hold,
insidious, as imperceptible
as thoughts unspoken, or a truth untold,

the first beginnings of self-censorship.
They worried about hierarchy and were
no longer Martian but a part of it.
Secure, and yet more subject now to fear,

they changed the oral levels they had scored
to fit an online test they didn't trust—
afraid superiors might be annoyed,
they compromised; and this, although unjust,

teachers began to live with, as men do.
And maybe there were students, one or two
whose *FANEV* blocked them from a post abroad
whose language ratings had been put too low

to satisfy a system teachers knew
flawed, but the current article of faith—
yet even as computer error grew
teachers became afraid to say the truth.

How is it that a hierarchy turns men
into executors of small routines,
middlings, whose benighted, lesser selves
wander a darkened world, mere hirelings—

in their appointed places, to ignore
the flare of first ambitions and the flame
a higher calling gave them, who they were
before the sad factotums they became?

Oh, sweet Aglaia, sorrowed in her grave
who lived and breathed a life in every breath,
who knew to wake the inner lives men have—
how could she have imagined living death?

How could she have imagined ardors dimmed,
and the once proud provocateur eclipsed,
how very careful teachers would become
to maintain reputations, and that this

poison would seep in slowly, chill the soul—
how could she, in these contracts won, project
a modern hemlock, a new way to kill
in bureaucratic meanness, or expect

teachers to lose the pride of who they were?
And so it is, how many battles fought
build but the prisons of a baser care—
what *quality of service?* Hours taught?

Evaluations at the end of year—
Had they fulfilled their duties, course creation,
quota of testing due? Had they supplied
their pound of flesh to an administration

counting what it can count—the measurable?
How could she have imagined the new mood,
the teachers' loss become unsayable,
servility become an attitude—

uneasy in her grave she knows it now.
Bitter, the revolution that gives rise
to this bootlick, fear-filled scenario,
and sweet Aglaia watching where she lies

abashed, as for a second time she dies,
sees that upon her grave no flowers grow.

# Death of an Adjunct

*Paris, France*

They told him he was out, no longer needed
after thirty-eight years, but he knew what they meant,
they wanted pure compliance, not a veteran,
someone who questioned less, an easy pass,
a body language that bespoke submission—
in brief, the administration knew best—
for who was he to doubt collective wisdom
of those who'd just arrived three months before?

I heard the story from someone I knew
who worked there too, but kept a low profile—
how many times the man had said much more
than anyone—at meetings he, alone,
dared still to look directors in the eye.
The best retreated to a neutral mien,
the worst sent body signals to conceal
the questioning in their hearts. Imagine them

around a table, twenty-odd or so,
nodding their heads in unison, abject,
a pantomime of furious consent,
as if an unseen hand held them in thrall—
something about mid-level civil servants
demands obeisance, hierarchical respect.

I sometimes wonder how, from what I know
he'd lasted there so long, and the mistake
of thinking who you are will still prevail
intact, no matter what those meetings cost,
because the way we've spent our days, somehow,
becomes an inner life, the one he'd lost

86

before he hanged himself in Room 16
choking upon its molded cornices,
his tongue now blackened, his unspoken spleen
taking a life that was no longer his.

# What Proust Would Do

*advice to a poet*

You should observe, the way he did
the microcosm that is yours,
the face averted of a friend
whose cause you once defended,
how suddenly you are unseen,
in *open office* spaces—
how fast a salaryman can glean
who is in whose good graces.

You should record, as if that world
awaits for you to live again,
minutiae of days endured,
betrayal by subaltern men,
the sad ballet of one success
their silences demean,
how conversations cease—at best—
when Arab at the coffee machine.

How new directors keep their doors
ajar, but their agendas closed,
assigning *road maps* and applause,
the unctuousness, the self-imposed
attentive mien and gladsome verve
that's de rigueur—*Good Practices*
defined as how employees serve
the serfdom of their offices.

And if, like him, you recreate
a world remembered to reveal
another truth as you translate
to metaphor what these men feel,

the labyrinth of little rooms
seen from within, a windowless place—
you may redeem the trivial,
a life no living can abase,

a mind observant, now set free
as if thick clouds laid overhead
parted, and far as eye can see
made visible the mind instead—
till resurrected to itself,
to wasted time half-reconciled,
it turns it into something else,
ageless, intact, and undefiled.

# A LIFE THAT IS

# Rainbows of Sky

One of the mysteries of life
is why the man at the counter
prints "TSA Pre-Check" or not
on my boarding pass. You wonder

was it deliberate or random—
how you chose someone, or didn't—
was there decision whenever
choices were made?

What's happened is like a portrait
whose brush strokes obscure the first draft—
or did the girl I've forgotten
believe she was calling the shots?

The trouble is, fixed agendas
can't bring her the great blue heron
striding the mudflats to meet her
evenings, alone.

The best thing about enigma
is this, that maybe tomorrow
someone like the TSA man,
an unexpected encounter,

surprises a habit of sorrow
the way the sun stripes the water
even at ebb tide, to borrow
rainbows of sky.

# The Problem with Masks

The problem with masks is I can't see your face,
you have to learn to smile with your eyes,
a body language of attentiveness
in these hard times—
I miss too all the signals the mouth gave
of falsity, of tentative deceit,
made visible in the angle of the lips
mind can't dictate.

We are all masked and enigmatic now,
it's hard to know what anyone is thinking.
The bad boys of my youth once taught me how
the mouth's the thing—
better to watch it for the first betrayal
infinitesimal movements, lips awry,
hypocrite, whose mask upon withdrawal
the lips belie.

But most of all I miss the human face,
its sudden inspirations, thoughtfulness,
the way it changes, like the changing light
in Paris streets,
the passingness of intimate emotions
mirrored but for a moment as it meets
another gaze, mouth winsome, and is gone
leaving no trace—

except in the cauldron of remembrance,
alchemy of longing, our regret,
the kind of thing we need to keep going
in spite of it.

# At the Market with Philip Roth

"Children are always disappointing,"
one friend announced.
And so are parents—expectations—
only the moment counts,
the "pointless meaningfulness of living,"
you say, and you are right.

The way the fish in rigor mortis
shine silver on the counter,
fruit overflowing in street markets,
figs bursting at the center,
the spectacle of their abundance,
seed-filled, in purple splendor.

Something about the saffron-colored
girolles piled up beside
eggplants, in polished black, and bulbous,
returns me to the world—
its cornucopia of things passing,
pointless, but what I need.

Because I want, despite the children,
disappointing or not,
this paean to the earth it raises
so many live without—
and every day a thing of beauty
I had not thought about.

# Dear Millennial

"The purpose of living," you ask, and "what's the point?"
It all seems useless to you looking forward
in instant algorithms, but it's after,
once you've weighed anchor, only from afar,
you see, the way the beveled cliffs of Dover
tower to their full height when you set sail.

I'm not a model, I have to admit.
I've turned down so many chances of living,
my house is cluttered with measuring cups a husband
gave me for Christmas, half of its windows
walled over in stone—what the French do
to lower their taxes. It's uncomfortable,

the questions you're asking, when the furniture
fills up the spaces that were once my own.
I'm not a role model, and I can tell you
things it wouldn't be good for you to hear,
the multiple selves I left disappointed
for you to bloom, how the sore heart pauses

because the mind it seeks is multitasking
each time I phone. It's true, I can't offer much,
the homilies successful people bring,
tweaking "commencements" to a grand rebirth—
their easy optimism is not my thing.
I know the beast that gnaws from underneath

remembering life before it has been lived,
time counted now against a drip-drop clock
no one can see.
                    Nevertheless, I think
how the light filters through the balsam fir,
gliding to morning as the fog lifts off,
gilding horizons, blanching the grass—

nothing of what you loved once has been lost.
Only the gladness of an open heart,
wonder, the surprises that keep me alive,
blossom, that sweeter impulse to impart
something within to these ungentle shores—

a life, my dear millennial, that's yours.

# Noces

*in difficult times, for H. from Camus*

It's about seeing in the vacant lot
beside the broken glass and paper clutter
a rhubarb plant, and how fenced earth begot
three poppies growing there beside the gutter.

How red their petals are against the grey
of lidded skies and days on end confined,
as if their luster promised to repay
the passerby who stopped, a life defined

not by relentless soliton-like days
mowing all whitecaps in fixed amplitude,
but by these crests of feeling as intense
as rhubarb sprouting doggedly, displays
of things so unexpected in our mood—
these poppies pushing three heads through a fence.

# In Defense of Dubai

Why didn't he put the buildings more spaced out,
you ask, and there are far too many—
He's overbuilt, utterly defied nature,
dredged from beneath the Arabian Sea
islands already sinking, done without
a hundred rules to bring Atlantis back—
Why didn't he think of aquifers, you ask,
sustainable development, the air
before he built those highways to the mall?

Sheikh Al-Maktoum is not an engineer—
A megalomaniac then, you say—
A poet, I reply, you might as well
expect a visionary to count beans . . .
I love the pink extravagance the isle
projects above the breakers, like a shell
laid on the sea, the pinnacle of towers,
the silver-fluted point *Burj Khalifa*
stabs at the sky. Something about the cranes,
nodding their heads or idle, I know means
reach, and do not despair—he speaks my language,
this sheikh that you and others would dismiss,
dreamer and architect of the inner life . . .

Tell me what poetry is, if not this—
the unconstructed castles of the mind
waiting to be built?

# The Internaut

You don't have to know everything that's happening,
yesterday, tomorrow, or in real time,
hashtags of causes, each of them competing
in loud verbatim. Listen to the trees,
breathe in the linden blossoms, rue Froidevaux,
the bakery exhaling, the charred smell
of chestnuts roasting boulevard Montparnasse—
and put away the easier paradigm,
       selfies for inner self.

After the morning grey, the afternoon
bursts through the clouds unfailingly: throughout,
suffused in gold, the city speaks, and soon
you'll hear the café terraces, the girl
plucking a harp in the maids' room upstairs,
the clink of dishes—but your days, unspent,
monitor vlogs that hold you in their thrall
because, you say, you're afraid of missing out—
       as if you haven't.

How is it that these words are not enough
to waken you to everything unsaid
that lingers still as if another life—
the city's breath, the city's beating heart,
its bridges reaching, sculptures half erased,
its barges sliding underneath their beam,
horns blowing, the sky lifting, and the start
of summer, when the poets you once read
       still made you dream?

# He Asked

He asked if it was true, love at first sight,
the tale she'd told before, when he was young,
and was this *coup de foudre* something like
the feeling he'd just had. He'd met someone—

Was it a sudden jolt of recognition
as if a tapestry hung on a wall
began unweaving and the person in it
stepped out, enlaced in lambent aureole

of blithe Annunciation? All his life
he'd loved the story. But she kept quiet,
not wanting him to question her, as if
her own belief, like his, depended on it.

The truth was somewhere else. As if the body
spoke in another language to the mind,
knowing how it lay fallow, and that she,
untouched for decades by a loving hand,

couldn't defend the history she'd concealed.
It's hard to live our knotted separate parts
as if they were one, harder still to shield
the young whose earnestness and yearning hearts

might do better with truth, nevertheless.
She knows this, but cannot bring herself to show
a hint of disillusion to unbless
the myths we try to live by anyhow.

Forgive her then, that she is bound by love
for you alone, to silence like a scream,
her body in the basement, and to move
dreams of enchantment to a safer room.

# At the Chateau de la Chatonnière

*for Béatrice de Andia*

What is it woke you to the land,
the hills that fall away to fields,
how to coax roses from the sand,
fertile the earth until it yields

gold-ripe or luminescent mauve
gardens of lettuces and beans?
And what lost passion is it gave
palatial appetites like these?

No matter how we understand
the human heart, upon these plains
of bowered walks, not Talleyrand
nor Cortes' blood still in your veins

will tell us more than poems unsigned
still whispering here from lavender
in amphitheaters of the mind
that you, and you alone, can hear—

A fragrant pergola of dreams
inhabited by you alone
and where the woven willow seems
to shield lush grasses still unmown.

These shapes, the colors, and the scent
of terraced garden against field
whose fierce geometry was meant
a contradiction to the wild

are outward signs of something bold,
a something tender but contained,
an inner paradox untold,
a life like mine, still unexplained.

# Ode to Silence

Here's to the silence of unspoken word,
the heart held in abeyance, like a clam,
shut tight against indifference, but still heard
by men who give these nameless things a name—

Who never watch reality TV,
nor rush to reconnect at Wi-Fi stations,
who apprehend implicits, and that we
lose them, in our *relationship discussions.*

Here's to the wordless hurts that do not whine,
begging for recognition, and remain
silent, as pulp psychologists opine
better for mental health that they complain.

Here's to the silence before SMS,
instant translator of our ups and downs,
became the inner life we could express
cheaply, before emoticons, like clowns

pulled a long face, exaggerated smile,
to summarize the soul. This age of noise,
"You should have had the balls to speak," this style
everyone shares, this feelingness that cloys,

like squeezing a banana in your fist—
This is the Age of Treacle, someone said,
and Facebook gripes. How has self come to this—
As if these tell-all postings, half-unread,

were proof of being? Let silence reign
in the unspeakable chasm they perceive,
mothers whose only gift from life is pain,
prodigal sons, lovers who cannot grieve—

Here's to the gated silence in the pause
poets can hear, while glib men only post,
what Beckett found in wordlessness, because
*saying nothing sometimes says the most.*

# Remote

*for H.*


I don't need an SMS to tell me,
a WhatsApp to forewarn,
e-mail, instant messenger, or FaceTime—
something's wrong.

I heard it in the rain that came this morning
three thousand miles from where
you go about the business of still trying—
I know you are

suffering, the same way trees are shaking
their last leaves to the ground,
windswept, bent over, the mind breaking—
a winter storm.

I hear beneath the blow and the cloud cover
darkening the sky
the moody aftermath of indecision
we both deny.

That's why it's a mistake to judge me clueless—
your doubts are mine—
outside, above the roof a jib crane reaches
across and down.

It makes me think of you, how hard to build
castles with this slow freight,
laborious, as if ambitions needed
a counterweight—

and wonder what would happen if its fulcrum
tipped, and its latticed mast,
its ballast not enough to hold it,
capsized and crashed.

I hear you in your silence hesitating
to hoist earth to the sky,
and measure when the jib arm stops rotating
your grief and why.

# The Pink House on the Rue Lagrange

The pink house on the rue Lagrange
whispers as I pass on
something I recognize, but strange,
muted, as if someone

faintly, behind its rose façade
calls me to who I am,
moves me as if I must decode
an urgent cryptogram.

As when a building or a view,
Sacré Cœur from Quai d'Orsay,
so unexpected, can make new,
unsaid, the everyday.

The pink house on the rue Lagrange
reminds me of lives wasted,
the alchemy we need to change
perceptions so distracted.

# Prayer for Writers

*for Patrick Modiano, Proust, and all the others*

An author we'd invited came to talk
after we'd read her book six months before.
Reviewing it, I was surprised, no mark,
made when a page is memorable, was there—

where words implode to breach another depth,
where images suspend in metaphor
a hanging garden, pages I collect
and mark to breathe again, to re-explore—

my pencil had marked nowhere to return.
Her book was action-packed, fast-paced, its prose
a page-turner, she said, as if to spurn
books that weren't that, Modiano, Proust, and those

"No one today has time to read," she said.
And in this glib dismissal of an art
of inner worlds beneath the esplanade
of surface, the meanderings of thought

that open to awareness all our own,
in this refusal of parentheses,
I heard her rule: the story must go on,
humdrum or not, with characters like these,
caricatures of their intrinsic selves,
made simple, Manichean to a fault.

May you, the Mrs. Dalloway of worlds
not yet our own, still give us to exalt
vast prairies where red poppies here and there
remind us of our losses, where the light,
breaking below the clouds, gilds to appear
rich as Duke Berry's days, our days re-thought—

Books that are never page-turners, but stop
time, as another consciousness, unfurled,
beckons across dim landscapes, conjures up
luminous days to resurrect a world.

# The Mind at Last

It's hard not to regret how time is passing,
the books unread, the paintings still unseen—
busy as if your life depended on it,
answering mail, installing Windows 10—
the noise of time that keeps us from ourselves.
As if the kitchen detail of our lives
cut time in little pieces, like church bells
sounding the end of hours no one grieves.

I want to be again someone I saw
walking in Baty square, a book in hand,
oblivious of the crowd, as pigeons scattered—
to hear again, above the noise, the call
of something vast, the way I'm sure he did,
the mind at last the only world that mattered.

# What I Miss

*after reading Magyd Cherfi's* Ma Part de Gaulois

It's hearing these hurt faces and the look
male-take-none-of-this-shit, when the police
stop for a "random" check—the universe
of coded words recaptured in this book—

The heartbeat of these lives lived in the projects,
concrete and syncopated, like a drum,
music of these street cadences become
an ache in me, a visceral poetics

I miss as much as them. I must go home
to hear again the old vernacular,
the metrics of what made me who I am,
the boys whose catcalls echo in the night,
whistling the girls, but wise enough to ask her:
"Hey, pretty dress, everything alright?"

I must go home again to get it right.

# About the Author

Athar C. Pavis grew up in New York City and studied literature in France. She lives both in Maine and in France where she has worked at the Ministry of Foreign Affairs and teaches at the Sorbonne. Her poems have been published in the UK, Canada, and in U.S. magazines, in *Able Muse, Five Points, Trinacria, The Comstock Review,* and *The Orchards Poetry Journal,* among others.